One happy hippo practicing Kung-Fu.

1

"Can I join you?" asked her brother Lou.

One hippo plus one hippo, that equals two.

Two happy hippos racing round a tree.
"Can I join you?" asked their neighbor Lee.

Two hippos plus one hippo, that equals three!

Three happy hippos playing grocery store.
"Can I join you?" asked their friend Theodore.

6

Three hippos plus one hippo, that equals four.

Four happy hippos doing fancy dives.
"Can I join you?" asked cousin Clive.

Four hippos plus one hippo, that equals five.

Five happy hippos rumbling in the sun.

They're running, rolling, riding...

they're playing till day's done.

1 + 1 + 1 + 1 + 1 = 5 happy hippos having tons of fun!

Addition

Add up every bicycle and add up every tree.
Add up every hippo. How many of each do you see?

Can you find any other sets to add?

addition Cheer

Hooray for Addition!

Let's clap and tap
and touch the ground.
Let's jump and thump
and spin around.
Let's romp and stomp
and cheer and shout
for something
we can't live without:
    ADDITION!